THE STORY OF
SANDY BELLS

Edinburgh's World Famous Folk Bar

GILLIAN FERGUSON

Matador
9 Priory Business Park,
Wistow Road, Kibworth Beauchamp,
Leicestershire. LE8 0RX
Tel: (+44) 116 279 2299
Fax: (+44) 116 279 2277
Email: books@troubador.co.uk
Web: www.troubador.co.uk/matador

ISBN 978 178462 100 1

British Library Cataloguing in Publication Data.
A catalogue record for this book is available from the British Library.

Every attempt has been made to contact copyright holders to use the
material for this publication in order to ensure proper attribution and
copyright information. Any inadvertent omissions will be rectified in
future editions if the sources become known.

Typeset by Troubador Publishing Ltd, Leicester, UK

Matador is an imprint of Troubador Publishing Ltd

This book is dedicated to my husband, Ian Ferguson, who keeps the Sandy Bells bar profits ticking over and keeps me warm at night.

CONTENTS

ACKNOWLEDGEMENTS

My grateful thanks go to the following people for their support, encouragement and help in my research for this publication: Charlie Woolley, David Cossar, Duncan Clark, Ian Green of Geentrax Recordings., John Groat, Keith Henderson, Michael Wiedenhof, Peter McClements, Robert Gold, Steven Hannah and the patrons of Sandy Bells.

PREFACE

Sandy Bells captured my imagination over three years ago when I first started attending the bar with my future husband and listened to tales of its rise to fame during the Scottish folk revival. My curiosity prompted me to seek out a publication about the history of Bells and I was disappointed when my search proved fruitless. This then became my inspiration to research and record the history myself and in doing so it soon became apparent that it was already becoming lost. It is perhaps fitting that my history was completed in the year that the bar celebrates 75 years of existence.

Gillian Ferguson
Edinburgh 2014

Quam Maxine
(as much as possible)

ONE

1800s to 1969

Sandy Bells is an unassuming little bar situated just a hop, skip and jump from Edinburgh's magnificent castle. A stranger could easily walk past the bar but this little gem is world famous and a Mecca for lovers of folk music from all over the globe. This is the extraordinary story of Sandy Bells' rise to fame.

The origins of Sandy Bells as an internationally known folk music bar go back to the late 1940's when the Theatre Workshop brought Ewan MacColl's plays as an unofficial contribution to the Edinburgh Festival and ran folk song events as side shows where the performers often found their way to Sandy Bells for impromptu performances. This grew into the first Edinburgh Peoples' Festival and the earliest manifestation of what was later to become the fringe. For several years folk music and ceilidhs were presented to the international public from Oddfellows Hall, almost directly across the road from Sandy Bells. In need of sustenance the performers crossed the road and crowded into Sandy Bells both before and after the performances and the bar resounded to singing and music. At these events notable singers Calum Johnston and Flora MacNeil sang Gaelic folk-songs, while John Strachan and Jessie Murray sang 'muckle songs' or 'big ballads'. Later they were joined, both in the shows and the bar, by Gaelic folk singers Kitty and Marietta MacLeod from Lewis and, representing the north east, Arthur Argo and Jimmy McBeath. Along with the music and singing, storytelling was a large feature of the entertainment and the bar patrons remained silent while listening intently to Scottish yarns.

With its close proximity to Edinburgh University and the Royal Infirmary, Sandy Bells became a medical school retreat as far back as 1947 and a melting pot of academics, writers, poets, artists, intellectuals, Gaelic speakers, story tellers, singers and musicians. Sandy Bells is near the School of Scottish Studies in George Square where international poet, song writer, intellectual and peerless collector of folk songs Hamish Scott Henderson (1919-2002) was the senior lecturer. Hamish was a stalwart of the Traditional Music and Song Association, mentor of folk music and a key figure in the Scottish Folk revival in the early 1950's where he provided the first public folk platforms to bring together traditional and revivalist singers. He was proud of his discovery of Jeannie Robertson and helped to inspire a new generation of singers, including Jean Redpath, Jimmie Macgregor and Josh McCrae. It was said that he operated a covert 'open door' policy at the School of Scottish Studies giving many vital access to materials even though they were not matriculated students, and he went on to inspire many folk singers.

Sandy Bells became Hamish Henderson's favourite 'howff' (a haunt or meeting place) and he regularly attended the bar in the company of his faithful dog Sandy. He often referred to Sandy Bells as his 'office' and recalled that 'often there were rows of people jammed tight between the alcoves and the arch listening to the singers and music and that those scenes in many ways

Jimmy McBeath, Willie Scott, Davie Stewart and Jeannie Robertson
Papier maché images by Jan Miller © Greentrax recordings

could be regarded as the culmination and high point of the first stage in the development of Sandy Bell's as a folk club-song pub'.

During this time a crowd of 'Teddy-boy bikers', most of whom were James Dean look-alikes with leathers and chains, started frequenting the bar. Hamish Henderson took them under his wing and encouraged their interest in music to the extent that the lads formed a skiffle group which certainly broadened the music sessions until their unruly friends became over-fond of consuming copious amounts of Bertram's Ales.

In 1958 the University Folksong Society was jointly founded by Hamish Henderson and Stuart MacGregor (1935-1973), who became its first President and used the bar as a base for folk music. At the time Stuart Macgregor was a medical student, poet, playwright, folk singer, and songwriter. It was the same year that Stuart wrote 'The Sandy Bells Man' which remains the bar's well known theme song.

The Sandy Bell's Man

It was early in May and the lilac smelt sweet,
I was strollin' one evenin' round town,
When I met a young maid over Morningside way,
And she sobbed as she hung her head down,
"I see by your scarf of the scarlet an' gold
An Edinbura medic are you
Come sit beside me come hear my sad tale
It concerns a young medic I knew"

Chorus:
My father's name was Harry,
My mother's name was Ann,
Come sit beside me come dry all my tears,
I've been wronged by a Sandy Bell's Man.

When I was sixteen, I was spotless and clean,
I had never tasted a drop
When I met a young medic, his name it was Derek,
He took me into that bad shop
And there on the nips of the whisky and gin
I verily drank my fill
My father he shot himself over my shame,
And my mother he likewise did kill

One day to my lover in haste I did go
And to him these same words I did say
"Oh my darling, I think that next summer or spring
An arrival is coming our way"
The whites of his eyes grew wide with surprise,
As the eyes of a young father will
But when I called round the next day at his digs
He'd had caught the first plane for Brazil

So come all ye virgins of Edinboro town,
Although you be ever so few
Come sit beside me, come hear the sad tale
That concerns the young medic I knew
Take warning, be warned before you be burned,
Fatal not yet is the hour
And next time a medical glances your way,
Be content with a hot an'cold shower

In 1967, aged 31 years Stuart wrote The Myrtle and Ivy, set in 1958 and within its pages Sandy Bells was thinly disguised as Connor's with many of the Sandy Bells' worthies appearing suitably disguised throughout the book. Hamish Henderson was thought to be Hector Gunn and Jeannie Robertson was Maisy May. The book was dedicated to 'the brotherhood of Sandy Bells – especially as it was then'. In the author's note, Stuart stated that the two great seats of learning in Edinburgh were the university and Sandy Bells.

In the 1960's Sandy Bells was well established as a folk/blues music venue where musicians and singers performed, encouraged by the bar managers. The cliental kept the noise level to a minimum while singers were performing but were more than happy to spontaneously join in a rousing chorus. At this time Sandy Bells was the only session bar in Edinburgh offering this type of entertainment and it was soon frequented by large numbers of people representing both Orkney and Shetland Isles who sought out the venue for traditional music. The bar's reputation grew until it became known worldwide and soon there was hardly a single figure of any importance in the folk scene on both sides of the Atlantic who had not frequented the bar at some point or another.

Among regular performers at the time were Paddie Bell of the Corries, The late Martyn Bennett, Jean Ritchie, Belle Stewart, Jean Redpath, Archie Fisher, Matt McGinn, Ali Donaldson, Danny Kyle, Gerry Rafferty, Bert Jansch, Isla St Clair, Mike Whellans, The McCalmans and Aly Bain who all fused their love of the traditional music there.

Visiting musicians and singers were encouraged to join in the regular sessions and Sandy Bells hosted groups as varied as The Clancys, The Dubliners, DeDannan, The Weavers, The Chieftains, and The Reivers. Towards the late 1960's Pete Seeger, Tom Paxton, Paul and Finbar Furey and Davy Arthur had played in Sandy Bells sessions and Billy Connolly enjoyed coming into Sandy Bells for the 'crack' as much as the music.

Sandy Bell's Bar is located at 25 Forrest Road, Edinburgh, EH1 2QH on the corner of Forrest Hill. The street was named after Sir James Forrest Bt, first Baronet of Comiston and Lord Provost of Edinburgh from 1837-43 ,who was remembered for blotting his civil copy book by falling asleep instead of welcoming Queen Victoria during her first visit to Edinburgh in 1842. The original thoroughfare was created in 1618 as an access to the Greyfriars Priory and it is possible that the site on which Sandy Bells now stands was originally the Franciscan Priory's physic garden. The rest of the area in 1647 was an open grass park. By the 1840s part of the Telfer wall was demolished to make way for the construction of Forest Road. During the excavations for the current building the labourers discovered bones and coffins only six feet below the surface from an ancient and forgotten cemetery.

The surviving East wing of the Edinburgh poorhouse (now flats) on Forrest Hill at the rear of Sandy Bells (right).

Only yards away from the remains of the Flodden wall, Sandy Bells adjoins the surviving East wing of the old charity poorhouse and parochial office, built between 1739 and 1743 and last documented in the Edinburgh and Leith Directory of 1869/70. Now converted into residential flats, the poorhouse had a strong box for donations at its gate inscribed 'He that giveth unto the poor lendeth unto the Lord'.

In the triangle between Forrest Road and Bristo Place, to the front of Sandy Bells, originally with the Telfer wall, stood Darien House. This was built to accommodate the headquarters of the ill-fated Darien scheme which sought to create a trading colony on the Isthmus of Panama, the demise of which saw Scotland facing financial ruin, contributing soon after to the Act of Union with England. The building became part of the lunatic asylum or 'bedlam' catering largely for the paupers in the adjoining workhouse. It was in the bedlam that one of Edinburgh's most famous and influential literary figures, the poet Robert Fergusson died on 16th October 1754 aged 24, having sustained a head injury after falling down a flight of stairs.

> *Reikie, farewell! I ne'er cou'd part*
> *Wi thee but wi a dowy heart*

Extract from Robert Fergusson's most famous poem, Auld Reikie 1773

Darien House has long since been demolished but some of the old bedlam buildings are incorporated in the Hotel du Vin and the name is preserved as the Bedlam Theatre which occupies the former New North Free Church on the apex of the streets.

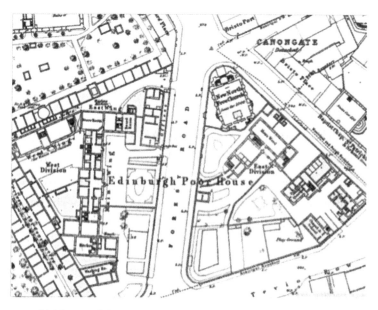

1846 map of Forrest Road showing the site of the poor house

According to the Edinburgh and Leith directory of 1874/5 the first entry for no. 25 Forrest Road was for Robertson, a grocer who resided at no 23. The premises passed later to W G McLeod and from 1926-29 became 'Jacks'. Mrs Mary C. Bell, who had previously been involved in a wine and spirits business in Leith Walk, bought the premises in May 1929 with a loan from the brewers T and J Bernard. The bar has been affectionately known as Sandy Bells from at least 1947 although it was officially called the Forrest Hill Bar until the name was formally changed to Sandy Bells by licensee, Charlie Woolley in the 1990's

But where did the name Sandy Bell come from? Who indeed was Sandy Bell? It is doubtful if we will ever know for certain so the name remains cloaked in mystery and rumour. Current suggestions are:

a)   Sandy Bell was a former licensee.

b)   Sandy was the barman who for many years rang the bell at closing time.

c)   Sandy Bell was the husband of Paddie Bell of the Corries who sang in the bar.

d)   Perhaps indeed Alexander (AKA Sandy) Graham Bell visited the bar in his twilight years and was partial to a dram or two while scribbling his invention on the back of a beer mat leaving behind his name and perhaps a new telephone!

However, it is most likely that the name derived during Mrs Bell's ownership when she employed a nephew of the Bell family called Sandy Porter who was head barman from the mid 1940's until 1960. In those days the bar was referred to as either Bell's or Sandy's until the two names became fudged over time and the name Sandy Bells evolved. Indeed a bar regular drew a cartoon of the portly Sandy in 1949 which was reproduced in the Sandy Bell's Broadsheet in 1977. Sandy Porter was traced through an Edinburgh Evening news feature promoting the Sandy Bells Ceilidh. The article was seen by his neighbour, Mr Archibald, who informed the newspaper of Sandy Porter's connection to the bar. The 86 year old Sandy Porter was then invited back to Sandy Bells for a presentation of a silver tankard by Scottish and Newcastle Breweries.

Mrs Bell died in 1960 and the bar was sold to Scottish Brewers who became Scottish and Newcastle Brewers a year later. The bar is currently owned by the firm G1 Group plc. From 1960 the bar was managed on behalf of the brewery by Johnny McKenzie followed by Jack Sinclair, Harvey I'Anson and Peter

Sandy Porter 1949: with kind permission from Sandy Bells Broadsheet

Biggs until Jimmy Cairney took over the reins during the early 1970s until 1980. Various shorter term brewery managers including Maureen Anderson and Mary came and went following Jimmy's death until Charlie Woolley became the licensee from 1987 until November 2007. He was followed by Tom Bird until June 2011 when Steven Hannah became the current licensee.

Sandy Bells is a typical traditional Scottish bar which differs from English public houses primarily because of different building traditions, laws and a preference of spirits over ales. In Scotland spirits were displayed in casks on a frame behind the bar called a gantry. Most Scottish bars after the 1880's consisted of a large room often situated on the ground floor of a tenement and barely distinguishable from the shops either side or often, as in the case of Sandy Bells, a shop conversion. A Scottish public house is generally referred to as a bar which comes from the late Victorian period referring to the counter over which the drinks were purchased and later used in Scotland to refer to the whole establishment. It is a literary quirk in the United Kingdom that public houses are known for the vanishing apostrophe in their names and Sandy Bells follows that format.

Sandy Bells is entered through a small vestibule to one room divided into distinct front and rear areas by a fine wooden Edwardian pedimented arch with a walled arch at the rear of the room with access to the toilets. Between 1952 and 1954 both the gantry and the bar were increased in length and extended past the wooden arch to their current location. By the 1970s, the wooden panel in the arch spanning the counter was replaced by a glass panel which opened up the view to the bar extension. Today, the interior of Sandy Bells is regarded as being an historic pub interior of regional importance and it still retains the original fireplace, gantry and wood panelling.

TWO

1970 to 1999

Sandy Bells became a social meeting point for the Scottish literati who came together for readings together with the musical performances. In 1970, Stuart Macgregor compared and performed at the first meeting of The Heretics, which had been founded in order to provide a forum for young poets, singers and musicians. These included Donald Campbell and Liz Lochhead writers Hugh MacDiarmid, Sorley MacLean and Iain Crichton-Smith and poet Norman MacCaig who were known to meet with Stuart for social evenings in Sandy Bells. Stuart continued to inspire the Scottish folk-song revival and regularly visited Sandy Bells until his departure for Jamaica in 1972 where he tragically died in a car accident on 25th January 1973 but his song, The Sandy Bells Man, which received its first performance in the bar, still lives on.

Among well known regular performers in the bar during this period were Cathal McConnell, Dougie McLean, Rod Patterson, Jack Evans, Jock Broon and Norman Chalmers together with fiddle players Derek Hoy and Peter McClements. At the height of the Folk scene Hamish Bayne and Tom Ward frequented the bar along with Boys of the Lough, Bob Bertram,

Alex Burns, Paddy Brock and Geordie Hamilton AKA 'the Duke' who is attributed with introducing Dick Gaughan to the Burns' song 'Westlin Winds'. "Peerie" Willie Johnson was equally at home in Sandy Bells playing jazz or Shetland fiddle music and other well known faces were Neil Munro, John James, Mick Broderick, Chuck Fleming, Ken Stott, Ronnie Jamieson, Willie Beaton, Mike Brennan, and Dennis Cairns along with Johnny McIntyre who was known in Sandy Bells for his fine repertoire of songs.

Session musicians and singers in Sandy Bells would regularly swop tunes and learn their craft from each another by performing together and friendships were made that continue to this day. Many went on to find fame after their musical apprenticeship in the bar including current star of the folk world, accordionist Phil Cunningham who honed his music in sessions in the bar. Phil took a sick day off school to record in a BBC live radio show but was unfortunately caught out as his teacher had listened to the programme! Phil was only 16 years old when he followed his elder brother, Johnny Cunningham of Silly Wizard into the Sandy Bells sessions and into the folk business. It is said that folk stalwart and regular contributor to Sandy Bells sessions, Arthur Argo, persuaded accomplished fiddler Aly Bain to quit his joiner's job in Shetland and come to the mainland to play professionally. With Arthur's encouragement, Aly played regularly in the bar sessions and went on to become one of Scotland's best known and finest fiddlers. Barbara Dickson was a civil servant who started singing in the Sandy Bells sessions during this time before going on to became an international star. According to his official web site, well known blues singer, Tam White made his musical debut in a skiffle group in Sandy Bells.

Current folk star Dick Gaughan performed in the bar during his early days as a singer and musician as did popular group Silly Wizard. The evergreen Jock Tamsons Bairns grew out of the Edinburgh band Chorda who played frequently in Sandy Bell's in the 1970s and included Rod Paterson (vocals, guitars), John Croall (whistle, bodhran), Norman Chalmers (concertina, accordion) and Adam Jack (fiddle).

During those days Scottish licensing laws were strict and it took until The Licensing (Scotland) Act 1976 for public houses to escape from the 10pm closure to opening all day and Sundays. The old opening hours were just not long enough for the musicians and singers who wanted to continue their music sessions so they would take their drinks and adjourn to a flat on the third floor at no. 47 Forrest Road where it is said Hamish Bayne, Tich Frier, Tom Ward, Gordon McCulloch, Aly Bain and Dick Gaughan lived at times. The flat soon became known as the 'madhouse'. Round the corner, four doors away, lived Derek Moffat, Ian Laurie and Jimmie Milne who regularly joined them to perform in sessions in their 'local'.

In 1970 the bar became well-enough known internationally for Danish television to record a documentary in Sandy Bells. The old cash register, ashtrays and cigarette smoke date the monochrome film and the dress reflected the era. After filming in the bar the film crew recorded the singers and musicians performing when they adjourned to a flat after closing time. The young McCalmans, Rab Noakes, Elish Moore, Harry Cullin, (later manager of the Oxford Bar, Edinburgh) Tich Frier, and Dick Gaughan were recorded among other performers.

In their wisdom the brewery keen to bring its public houses forward into the 20th century decided that the removal of the arch would benefit the look and ambiance of the bar and it was earmarked to go. The regular patrons were so incensed at the sacrilege that Hamish Henderson organised a petition which when presented to the brewers finally put a stop to destroying the arch although it is believed to have been removed for a short period and stored in the cellar before being reinstated. Later, the brewery chose to give the bar a lick of paint during the period of the 1973 Edinburgh festival when the bar was normally packed with customers, visitors and full of festival venue posters. The posters had to be removed and were replaced by 'a standard war department' cream paint and the customers were invited to share the aroma of paint at the bars' busiest time.

Dick Gaughan wrote of Brewery 'crimes' in the Broadsheet

The fine Edwardian arch reinstated. © Gillian Ferguson

on 17th June 1976. "Everyone is aware of the death of the 'local' at the hand of the large monopoly Brewers and the devious methods employed in achieving this: Removal of darts, dominos and their replacement by wide-mouthed, coin swallowing fruit machines. Then as old regulars drift elsewhere, the Brewery claims that there is no demand for the pub and its present state and redecorate it then tear into what the image will attract a 'better class of drinkers' turning it into a plastic imposed semi-bordello, complete with muzak to dissuade conversation and to entice the teeny pop half pint wonders. It could never happen to Sandy Bells we all thought but look around you. Where are the old regulars? Where is the crack? Where is Sandy Bells internationally famous and hallowed bar? Sandy Bells used to be the only democratic pub in town where the regulars, the people who really count, dictated the rules, for what Scottish Brewers ever spend on the place; they get greater return than any other pub in town".

20th August, 1973 gave birth to the Sandy Bells Broadsheet, the brainchild of Dr John Barrow who jointly edited it with police officer, Ian Green and journalist and feature editor of the Daily Record, Kenny Thomson. Together, the three editors became known as the 'Triumvirate'. The Broadsheet was published fortnightly for Scotland's traditional music scene with the aim 'to communicate and by communication to draw the Scottish scene closer together so that it would become a unit without federation'. The first issue of one page appeared on 20th August 1973 priced 2p and was Scotland's only national folk magazine. The general format of the broadsheet was current news on the front page, 'Sandy Bell says' followed by 'you write', club round up, feature articles, gigs advertisements and on the back page 'we hear' folk news snippets. Issue nine, which was the first Christmas issue, was called 'Jingle Bells'

Regular editors' meetings were held over a dram or two in Sandy Bells while the trio gleaned every source of information from the bar luminaries. Armed with three portable typewriters, copious amounts of correction fluid and Letraset the issues were painstakingly typed up at home before being printed, hand folded and despatched. By the 14th issue in 1974 the editors were appealing for an electric typewriter up to £20! The caricatures were drawn by Tash MacLeod and humorous cartoons of Mike Brennan, Ray Fisher, Bobby Eaglesham, Dick Gaughan, Mike Whellans, Paul Furey, Bill Barclay, Danny Kyle, and Freddie Thomson along with the editors soon graced the pages. Malcolm McCormick who was known for the 'Tellytoons' and 'The Big Yin' cartoons in the Sunday Mail later made contributions to the broadsheet.

Despite its success and demand the Broadsheet ran on a shoe string and was often subsidised from the editors' pockets. It was not envisaged to make money and ran to provide a service but it often encountered financial difficulties, primarily due to cash flows while waiting for advertisers' payments. In 1976 in order to keep the publications going, three concerts were staged where the venues and all the performers kindly offered their services free to aid the publication. Some of the performers who gave their services included Aly Bain, Dick Gaughan, Chorda, the McCalmans, Liz and Maggie Cruickshank, the Bells Chorus, the Bells Big Ceilidh Band and the Melville Folk Group.

The pages of the publication expanded and the first photographs appeared in the Broadsheet on 13th December 1975 showing the presentation of the Sandy Bells Broadsheet Cup to

Hamish Henderson on 5th December 1975 with John Barrow, Ken Thomson, Jimmy Cairney and Ian Green.

In 1977 Sandy Bells Broadsheet Tee shirts were launched with a facsimile of the front page and a picture of Sandy Bells on the front priced £1.80. That was followed a year later with the 30cms black and white seven page Broadsheet calendar depicting both Broadsheet issue and folk festival dates.

Over time Sandy Bells Broadsheet had been mistakenly called Sandy Bells Broadside, John Barrows Tyneside and Drew Harris of Radio Clyde stopped short of calling it Sandy Bells Breadsheet on air. Such was the success of the Broadsheet that by the 8th year the international demand saw copies being despatched as far as Canada, USA, Sweden, South Africa, Eire, Germany, Holland, Belgium, Switzerland, Denmark, Saudi Arabia, Norway, Bermuda and France.

The regular advertisement for Sandy Bells was 'There's always good crack at Sandy Bells Forrest Hill Bar, 25 Forrest Road, a Scottish and Newcastle House. Manager: James Cairney: Where the folk all meet'. Ken Thomson left the Triumvirate in 1981 due to other commitments and Ian Green and Dr John Barrow continued editing for another year. Due entirely to editors' hard work and innovation the broadsheet ran successfully for nine years and 250 issues until the final issue on 13th September 1982 which was then priced 20p. The Broadsheet had become so well known that STV recorded a documentary on the life of the Sandy Bells Broadsheet. The Sandy Bells Broadsheet then became The Broadsheet under Jack Foley and the involvement with the bar ceased. It later moved to Aberdeen under Iain McDonald and became Broadbeat.

The Edinburgh Folk Club, founded by the Sandy Bells

Broadsheet editors and Sid Kidman first opened its doors on 3rd October 1973. It was held in the basement of the Roman Catholic Chaplaincy Centre at 23 George Square, only minutes away from Sandy Bells. As the venue was unlicensed its patrons would head for Sandy Bells during the interval for liquid refreshment and with the warmth of a dram or two often forgot to return to the club.

Along with editing the Broadsheet and being a founder member of the Edinburgh Folk Club, Ian Green is known for staging Irish group Clannad's Edinburgh debut, setting up the Edinburgh Police Folk Club (AKA Fuzzfolk) and later forming Greentrax Recordings Ltd. He has been featured in the Scottish Television Artery series and presented with The Hamish Henderson Award for Services to Scottish Traditional Music in 2005.

Dr John Barrow was also the first Artistic Director of the Edinburgh Folk Festival and held his first press conference in Sandy Bells in Jun 1978

The Sandy Bells Broadsheet Cup was generously donated by bar manager, Jimmy Cairney in 1974 to be awarded annually to an individual, a club, famous name, unsung hero, group or institution who had contributed significantly to folk music and the Broadsheet editors had the daunting task of requesting nominations.

The first recipient of the trophy was James Elliot, aged 64, known then as 'the Father of music' in Sandy Bells. Unpaid, Jimmy played jigs and reels and jazz on his guitar regularly in Sandy Bells and is remembered well for encouraging folk music. He was featured in the Scottish & Newcastle Brewers house paper as well as Sandy Bells Broadsheet. The cup was presented to the winners with a keepsake replica of the trophy and a bottle of whisky. The complete list of the cup winners were:

1974 James Elliot: Inspirer of music in Sandy Bells and brought the Bells Big Ceilidh Band

1975 Hamish Henderson: For nurturing and promoting the Scottish folk revival

1976 Tom Anderson: Fiddler: and President of the Traditional Music Song Association

1977 The Fisher Family: Well known family of traditional folk singers

1978 The Topic Records Company: Held a vast collection of British recorded folk music

1979 Alistair Clark: Of the Scotsman Publications and erudite chronicler of folk music

1980 Alex Campbell: Musician and ambassador of folk song

1981 Kenny Thomson: Promoting folk music and Chairman of Edinburgh Folk Club

1983 Eric Bogle: Folk singer/writer who wrote 'And the band played Waltzing Matilda'

1986 Nora Devine: Promoter of folk music who ran Linlithgow Folk Club for many years

1987 Arthur Johnstone: Political folk singer who ran the Star Folk Club in Glasgow

1988 The McCalmans: Successful group; Ian McCalman, Derek Moffat and Hamish Bayne

1989 Adam McNaughton: Folk singer, songwriter and humorist from the 1960s

1990 The Singing Kettle; Promoters of children's folk music. Awarded MBE

1992   Aly Bain: Well known accomplished Shetland fiddler

The Sandy Bells Broadsheet cup therefore continued to be awarded for services to folk music for ten years after the broadsheet stopped publication from Sandy Bells.

The Sandy Bells Ceilidh was recorded in the bar and Pan Audio Studios in 1977. The record album notes were compiled by Hamish Henderson. Greentrax Recordings re released the recording on cassette tape donating the proceeds to the Sandy Bells Broadsheet and the Living Tradition. A CD was subsequently launched and is currently available from Greentrax and Sandy Bells bar for purchase.

The album consisted of 13 tracks featuring regular musicians and singers in Sandy Bells many of who have since found fame in the folk scene. The album tracks are:

Side 1.

1. Hornpipes, An Comhra Down, The Galway, The Stand-Bells Big Ceilidh Band
2. John Barleycorn – The McCalmans
3. Fort Charlotte/Calum Donaldson – Aly Bain
4. The Lea Rig – Chorda
5. The Cruel brother – Dick Gaughan
6. Lowlands Away – Bell's Chorus

Side 2.

1. Sandy Bells Man – Liz & Maggie Cruickshank
2. Kirsteen – The McCalmans
3. Crossing the Minch – Aly Bain
4. Johnny Sangster – Chorda
5. Sleepy Toon – Dick Gaughan
6. Doon in the Wee Room – Bell's Chorus
7. Jigs: The Living fisherman, Lough Gowna, Sweet Biddy Daly-Bell's Big Ceilidh Band

The Bells' Big Ceilidh band consisted of the late Jimmy Elliot playing mandolin, Jimmy Greenan playing whistle, Jock Brown on tenor banjo with Adam Jack, Ian Hardie and Peter McClements playing fiddle. Norman Chalmers played concertina, Iain McNair and Allan Johnston guitar, with Roy Martin strumming bass, Rod Paterson shaking bones and John Croal and David Baillie on bodhran. The Bells Chorus consisted of the bar regulars in fine voice who frequently joined in music sessions regardless.

By 1977 there was a decline in traditional music and three local folk clubs shut their doors forever. Bar manager, Jimmy Cairney was concerned and anxious to enliven the bar to what it

Sisters, Liz and Maggie Cruikshank, singers of the Sandy Bells Man

had been formally. Sadly, ill health prevented him from fully accomplishing this mission.

Jimmy Elliot, former winner of the Sandy Bells cup, died on 18th February 1978 age 66 on his way home to the Southside after leaving Sandy Bells. Jimmy played guitar and mandolin and was the hub man of hundreds of sessions in the bar and was sadly missed. In his memory the Jimmy Elliot Memorial Concert was held on 16th May in the Usher Hall compared by Bill Barclay and featuring Boys of the Lough, Dick Gaughan, Bells Big Ceilidh Band and Mike Harding with the proceeds of the concert going to Jimmy's widow.

Following the concert, the Jimmy Elliot Memorial Society, J.E.M.S., was set up in May 1978 in order to help Scottish Folk musicians and their dependants in need. The officials were Chairman Harry Dawson, Vice Chairman Ronnie Lamb, Secretary Rod Patterson, Treasurer Ian Hewitt and committee members Adam Jack, Jane McRae and Barry Cormack (AKA Barry Feedback). In memory of Jimmy, the bar donated a James Elliot trophy to be awarded to instrumental pairs at the Kinross Festival.

A dozen or so figurines featuring some of Bells' worthies and musicians were made in self drying clay by John Forrest, one of the bar patrons. These we displayed behind the bar and over the course of years gradually disappeared as customers moved on. The last remaining figure still displayed on the gantry is of the late Jimmy Elliot and it is perhaps fitting that in a way he has never left the bar...

The Forest Hill Bar was closed for renovations after 10pm on 6 August 1978 until 5pm on August 17th. The new design was the brain child of Scottish and Newcastle Breweries who replaced the lighting with pink fluted shades and had the ceiling painted

Aly Bain and Jimmy Elliot
© Jim Irvine

crimson edged in white. The curtains were removed and replaced with new eye level shutters with logo transfers of red and gold on the window pane above. The locals were aghast at seeing a big expanse of window and likened it to a gypsy caravan. The plywood covering the gantry top was removed and copper and brass measuring jugs and imitation spirit casks were lined along the top to the consternation of the regulars who summed up the improvements as being akin to 'a job lot purchased from a house of ill repute in Danube Street!' Other regulars thought their bar looked like an ice cream parlour and were relieved that the cosmetic surgery stopped short of carpeting, a juke box and a one armed bandit. Jimmy Cairney often quoted 'This place is full of revolutionaries who want nothing to change'. The bar top was replaced and at least one improvement was well received by the locals. In their wisdom Scottish and Newcastle brewers installed an 'all glitter and gilt' clock whose exposed hands were often turned back by the regulars to improve the licensing laws even further despite Sandy Bells just being granted a 12 hour licence at that time!

The celebrations for the bar's 50th anniversary ran over four days commencing with a Golden Jubilee ceilidh held in the Friary, Bristo Street on Friday 25th May 1979 with the bar and raffle provided by Sandy Bells. Celebrations continued in the bar over the four days. A football match between the Edinburgh folk clubs and the Sandy Bells regulars resulted in a score of 8-5 to Sandy Bells before rain stopped play on the meadows. The jubilee was featured on BBC TV Reporting Scotland on the final day of the celebrations when former barman, Sandy Porter then aged 88 and Hamish Henderson were interviewed at the bar. Jimmy Cairney, Bill Barclay and Sandy Porter cut the celebration

Jimmy Greenan, Johnny Cunningham and Iain Grant
© Jim Irvine

birthday cake provided by Scottish and Newcastle Breweries
which was later donated to the sick Children's hospital.

Jimmy Cairney who had been manager of the bar for well
over ten years died on 25th May 1980. The bar was closed all day
on the 29th May out of respect while over 200 people attended
his funeral. During Jimmy's illness the bar had been run by a
succession of different managers from the brewery. The initial
managers were good but some lacked Jimmy's enthusiasm and
knowledge of folk music. At the time the bar was being promoted
as one of Scottish and Newcastle's 'Welcome Inns' and often the
Brewery tried to dictate the bars' needs and the music and the
bar started to decline.

On 25th January 1982 the Sandy Bells Broadsheet headline
ran 'Bells Bandit Outlawed'. The locals were outraged once again
when the Scottish and Newcastle Brewery proposed to install a
'one armed bandit' or puggie near the entrance to the bar. The
brewery had previously upset the regulars in 1975 when they

attempted to install a fruit machine which resulted in a 200 signature petition being presented to them. Perhaps, indeed the Brewery anticipated that in the seven years the locals would have mellowed. Despite this the 'bandit' was duly installed on 6th May 1982. The only player was a barman who barely had time to lose £2.40 before the unwelcome machine was uplifted and 'poltergeisted 'into the street by the outraged cliental.

Local worthies still recall the event but time often diminishes memories and to this day some swear it was a fruit machine that was jettisoned while others insist it was the a wall mounted juke box. A former barman recalls on the web 'I remember, many years ago, just after a new manager had taken over, he decided that what this dirty old drinking man's pub needed was a bit of 'culture', so he ordered a 'TV'. So the TV just arrived out of the blue one day, the locals had not been consulted. So when the men came in and plonked the TV down on the counter, the locals looked at each other, picked the TV up and just dumped it out on the street, saying' 'it's it or us'! There is no doubt that it happened and perhaps it was indeed a juke box, fruit machine and a television that met the street at various times. Needless to say, currently Sandy Bells does not have any of these items in the bar.

Highland piper, composer, and one of the best known Scottish 'moothie' players, Iain Grant faithfully led a music session every Sunday in the bar for some years. A stalwart of Scottish folk music Iain was an amazing player on a six key multiple diatronic mouth organ. In honour of Hamish Henderson he wrote a pipe march 'Dr Hamish Henderson' among other compositions. Sadly, Iain Gant died suddenly on 24th September 2003 aged 73 years. His compositions were played at his funeral and then the mourners congregated in Sandy Bells. Iain is still immortalized in a painting currently hanging on the wall of Sandy Bells.

> *He was Maestro of the moothie*
> *H'd sook and blaw a' day*
> *Wi' his pipe and dram before him*
> *For hours and hours he'd play*

A short extract from the 'Farewell to Iain Grant' composed by
Tom McAweany in memory of Iain.

The regulars in Sandy Bells were a force to be reckoned with when it came to changes to their 'boozer' but Ian Green recalled in his biography 'Fuzz to Folk' of the time when he put his head

Iain Grant
© Jim Irvine

in the door of the bar and asked for helpers to move chairs from the Festival Club in Chambers Street to a new venue. The bar emptied and the chairs were moved. Two similar scenarios showing the generosity of the regulars occurred years apart. The Old Town Housing Association raised a cry for help requiring volunteers to deep-clean the Trades Hostel for the homeless. True to form the regulars turned up in force and completed the job. More recently, large packages of timber were delivered at the main door of a flat and the occupier required help to move the timber up flights of stairs. The regulars left their pints, did the lift and went back to the bar to resume their drinks. The time span between these incidents involved different regular drinkers in the bar but such is the friendliness in Sandy Bells that the current regulars would, if asked, do it again tomorrow.

Irish group Planxty, the Bothy Band and singer and guitarist, Ken Stott, were all seen in Sandy Bells by 1982 together with the Easy Club who were formed from musicians playing in Sandy Bells who embraced modern styles and ideas into traditional music.

Some of the folk musicians had moved away to other venues during the inconsistency caused by a succession of temporary bar managers. When Charlie Woolley became the next long term licensee in 1987 he was anxious to encourage folk musicians back into the bar so Charlie engaged the successful Orkney born twins, fiddler Jennifer and guitarist, Hazel, known collectively as the Wrigley Sisters to play on Monday evening sessions. This was just a start and Charlie kept the bar together and took over the reins successfully where the late Jimmy Cairney left off and the bar began to progress and prosper once more under his guidance. A story is recounted during Charlie's time of when the bar cleaner

Entertainer, Andy Chung with former licensee Charlie Woolley
© Vivian Ramsay

discovered a pair of false teeth sitting in a yogurt carton on top of the bar. A while later the telephone rang and it was Hamish Henderson enquiring if he had left his teeth in the bar which were duly returned to a grateful Hamish!

Indeed the media has not overlooked this famous bar and many newspaper articles and films were produced about Sandy Bells which included international star, Emylou Harris who was filmed singing in a Sandy Bells session during her world tour in the early 1990's.

By the late 1990s folk singer and fiddler, Anna-Wendy Stevenson, Nuala Kennedy and Kris Drever played together in the Friday night sessions in Sandy Bells and they subsequently formed the group Fine Friday which produced two acclaimed albums and toured Europe and Australia. Anna-Wendy wrote 'I have drawn inspiration from various locations, architecture, festivals, but most of all from people I've met through my musical life, such as Edinburgh's famous Sandy Bell's pub'.

By the time the century was drawing to a close the bands Shooglenifty and the Peatbog Fairies could be heard playing in Sandy Bells and Tony McManus was also a regular player in the bar while singer and guitarist, Debra Cowan held a six month residency session during this time.

THREE

THE NEW MILLENIUM ONWARDS

Robert Gold, a young American journalist worked behind the bar for a year in 2001. On returning to the United States he wrote a fine article depicting Scottish pubs as social centres and recalling his memories of the Sandy Bells' worthies. The article, published by the Holland Sentinel newspaper in Michigan inspired two Americans to journey to Scotland to seek out the famous bar. They had such a good time visiting Sandy Bells that they donated the newspaper article which graced the bar notice board until the recent renovations.

In honour of Hamish Henderson, known as 'the founding father of the Scottish folk revival' the Carrying Stream Festival, (which was named after a line in Henderson's last poem, 'Under the earth'), was organised by the Edinburgh Folk Club with support from Edinburgh City Council. It was held over four days commencing in November 2002 during the week he would have attained his 83rd birthday and intended to be run annually during his birthday week. Among the events was a reception in Sandy Bells. The festival organisers commissioned Jan Miller to create a fine bust of Hamish out of papier mache from pages of his books and the sculpture was displayed above the gantry in

The papier mache bust of Hamish Henderson
© G Ferguson

Sandy Bells for some years beside an empty bottle of Lagavulin single malt whisky which was his favourite tipple. Sadly for Sandy Bells the bust was relocated after 2007 and can now be viewed in the National Museum of Scotland in the 'Scotland: A changing Nation' gallery.

Accomplished guitarist and multi-instrumentalist, Michael Wiedenhof, who has been Sandy Bells' head barman since 2002, recounted when Norwegian Blind Date filmed an episode in the bar. Set to impress his date the suitor was dressed in a gaudy snakeskin kilt. His manner was as loud as his outfit so his embarrassed date duly ignored him and remained at the bar conversing with the bar staff for the duration of the filming. Michael also recalls bar regular, Tom Flannigan, a double amputee who would often remove his legs to relax in the bar, being offered a lift at short notice to Auchtermuchty. Tom was on his way to the folk festival when the bar staff discovered his legs with a note affixed to them 'Send me to Auchtermuchty!'

Michael remembers famous violinist Sir Yehudi Menuhin,

Ali Donaldson (AKA William Mysterious) of Rezillos punk rock band, Ian McLeod of Shooglenifty, Comedian Phil Kay and Robin Morton, formally of Boys of the Lough and founder of Temple records coming into the bar. He has also served blues guitarist, Lorne Eldridge and writer Dylan Moran.

By 2005 Fine Friday group had disbanded and Kris Drever then teamed up with Sandy Bells associates, fiddler Aidan O'Rourke and accordionist Martin Green to form the successful folk group Lau.

In November 2005 Sandy Bells was chosen from more than 100 bars throughout the country to receive the McEwans' 'Session venue of the year award'. The award was launched by brewers to recognise Scotland's pubs which do the most to encourage

Head barman Michael Wiedenhof behind the bar
© Gillian Ferguson

traditional music as an initiative to bring more live music to the
nation's bars. The award ceremony was the centrepiece event in
a week of St Andrews Day celebrations being held in Edinburgh,
broadcast by BBC Radio Scotland.

Sandy Bells remains one of the few traditional pubs still
surviving in the city and it is still very much a local pub or
'boozer' as well as being a tourist attraction. It retained popular
bar activities which at one time included a domino team. The
Sandy Bells chess club included well known players Geoff
Chandler and Keith Ruxton who were authors of 'Rampart
Chess'. Other members included Mark Monaghan, M Rattery, E
Perry, Mark Condie, Joe Middleton and Robert Burns. The
Grangemouth premier and the premier Edinburgh congress were
among some of the leagues won between 2005 and 2007. The bar
still retains a trophy 'Chess on a summer's day 2002'. The Sandy
Bells chess club had three divisions, 1st, 2nd and 3rd (known as
turds by the regulars). Due to its success and promotion in the
Edinburgh league the Sandy Bells Chess club outgrew the space
in the bar and moved to different premises. Currently it is not
unusual to see casual chess or card players being serenaded by
music in Sandy Bells. John, a head bar man at the time,
successfully put together a team of cricket players from the
regulars who played in friendly matches. The historic Scotia bar
(established 1792) and the Glasgow Victoria bar, both centres for
folk music in Glasgow combined with Sandy Bells to host each
other's patrons' bi-annually. Friendly football matches were
played on the Edinburgh Meadows during the day and the
evening saw both pub members sharing drams and stories.

Phil Cunningham presented the documentary called
'Scotland's Music 'directed by Janice Hopper for BBC 2. The

Peter Vann, barman outside Sandy Bells: oil painting by Gillian Ferguson

documentary of six one hour long episodes told the history of Scotland's music from its roots to the present day. Part of the first episode 'Pride and Passion' broadcast on 17th November 2007 was filmed in Sandy Bells with Barbara Dickson (vocals and guitar) singing Riggs of Rye accompanied by Phil Cunningham (accordion), Troy Donockley (Guitar) and Aly Bain (fiddle).

Credit must go to bar licensee, Charlie Woolley who retired in 2007 after 20 years of revitalising the music sessions and nurturing Sandy Bells with a fair and firm hand. He still attends the bar and is well remembered for reminding people of differing ideas that 'this is a boozer son!!!'

Among many other characters over the years who frequented the bar, Tommy Hill, a self employed French polisher whose day off was a Monday, is remembered for being the founder member of 'the Monday Club' where regular patrons of the bar met up during the day to converse over a drink or two. Kenny McCoy, known as 'Newkie' for his fondness for Newcastle Brown Ale departed to live in New York and is remembered by the words and music of 'Kenny McCoy's Farewell to Sandy Bells', which was written and signed by Tom Flannigan and is currently displayed on the bar wall. Tommy and Kenny still come into the bar whenever they can. Former seaman, John Groat has attended the bar for many years.Since his retirement he is currently the 'Luther in residence' and is sought after by session musicians to repair their instruments so it is not unusual to see fiddle bow tubes left behind the bar. John, an accomplished musician can often be heard playing the mandolin on Monday evenings.

By May 2008, Sandy Bells had been named as one of the top five city attractions along with the castle and the Royal Yacht Britannia in that year's edition of the Lonely Planet's Scotland guide book. Furthermore, The Good Pub Guide notes that the traditional folk music department at Tokyo University recommends Sandy Bells to students visiting Scotland.

Famous people still drop into Sandy Bells. Eric Idle, of Monty Python fame while visiting Edinburgh for his production of Spamalot at the Edinburgh Playhouse in 2010 enjoyed the hospitality of Sandy Bells so much that he played the bar's guitar and remained in the bar well into the 'wee small hours', flaunting one of Sandy Bells tee shirts upon departure. The next day some of the regulars, who had shared the previous evening with Eric, were delighted to hear that he had generously donated free tickets for the opening night of Spamalot as he enjoyed their company so much. A kind gesture, indeed.

Scottish Television on 25 April 2012 gave a favourable résumé on Sandy Bells ending that it had 'become a legend in its own opening time'. Also in 2012 Antonio Forcione and the cast of Mother Africa were filmed in Bells. Indeed Muriel Gray has featured Sandy Bells in an article in The Scots Magazine.

Kevin McKidd, well known actor of the films Trainspotting, Rome and Grays Anatomy lived in a flat above Sandy Bells when he was a drama student in the mid 1990's. He passionately loved folk music and frequently attended the Bar in those days and returned to visit to his old haunt in June 2013.

Sandy Bells had somewhat declined over the last few years and the gantry was sparse. Regulars were often heard quietly singing the opening lines of Slim Dusty's song 'A pub with no beer'. In those days there were three types of cheap wine, red, white and take it or leave it. Steven Hannah, the current licensee came to the bar in June 2011 from successfully managing the Auld Toll pub in Tollcross and was previously responsible for the concept, design and refit of the Holyrood 9a public house upgrading it to be one of the most successful pubs in the chain. With the experience of revitalising a tired old pub under his belt Steve soon commenced upgrading Sandy Bells starting with a cosmetic makeover to the outside of the bar. The old red paint was substituted by blue which resulted in the regulars referring to the pub as 'Bluebells' for a while.

The gantry stock and ales grew like 'Topsy's nose' and the folk music sessions thrived under Steve's encouragement. The sign over the door of the pub reads 'Whisky Merchants' and indeed the gantry reflects the sign outside and by 2014 the bar

The newly painted 'Bluebells'
© Gillian Ferguson

boasted a fine selection of malt whiskies including 19 Speyside, 24 Highland, 3 Lowland, 11 Islay, 1 English, 3 Cambletown, 2 Edinburgh, 1 Indian and 3 Japanese. There is also an increasing good variety of other spirits. Currently there are 13 permanent draught beers, ales or cider, including , Tennent's Lager, Caledonia Best, Guinness, Budweiser Budvar, Innis & Gunn Lager, McEwan's Red, Schiehallion, Addlestones Cloudy Cider (Cask), Deuchars IPA, Bitter & Twisted, House 80/-,Ossian and a changing guest ale. Scottish styles of ales break down into Light, Heavy and Export. In 19th century Scotland, a nomenclature, based on the now obsolete shilling currency, was devised in order to distinguish between ales. 60/-was light, 70/- heavy, 80/- export, 90/- to 160/- for Scotch Ales.

Licensee Steven Hannah and barman Neil serving behind the bar

Indeed the selection in the bar continues to grow. Steve also introduced a coffee machine, toasted sandwiches, hot soup and homemade steak and ale pies to the menu.

On 5th January 2014 the bar was closed until 1st February for renovations and the folk music was silenced for three weeks. When it reopened the ladies' toilet had been removed and a new disabled/ladies toilet was built in the area formally occupied by the office. A second new ladies toilet was installed and the gents had a full makeover. This increased the area under the rear walled arch which is now generally used by the musicians at session times. The floor and lighting were replaced and the bar and gantry stripped and re varnished to reveal the wood grain once again. The frosted glass in the vestibule door was replaced by clear glass giving a view into the bar and plans to have a fuel fire restored are still in the offing. The renovations vastly improved the facilities while retaining most of the original features of the 140 year old building and, more importantly, its character.

Sandy Bells has an allure to it and over time people from all walks of life have been inspired to immortalize it in their own way. Well published poet, Norman Mc Craig OBE wrote 'Edinburgh Stroll'. The poem depicts the journey from Tollcross to Sandy Bells ending with the lines 'Tollcross to Sandy Bells bar, a short walk with a long conclusion'. Novelist and poet, Sydney Goodsir Smith penned Carotid Cornucopius' where Sandy Bells is referred to as 'Sunday Balls in Fairest Redd'. Magician Len Edwards, who enjoyed a pint of Deuchars ale in the bar, named his card trick 'the Sandy Bells shuffle'. The Sandy Bells Hornpipe was written in honour of Sandy Bells by Shetlander Rob Smith while at Edinburgh University in the early 1970s and recorded by groups Hom Bru, Blackeyed Biddy and Kevin MacLeod. Sam Aitken, an MA graduate in screen writing, commenced filming a documentary about Sandy Bells. Richard Demarco CBE painted 'Sandy Bells at Forrest Road' which is currently in the City of Edinburgh art collection. The author has completed three oil paintings featuring the bar exterior, the 'Itchy Scratchy Session' slow fiddle session and barmaid, Brittonie Fletcher behind the bar. Brittonie, an MA graduate in Fine Arts from Edinburgh College of Art photographed and developed portraits of the current locals for her degree show and her photographs currently grace the back walls of the bar.

Recently, a famous impressionist, a well known crime novelist, and a Nobel Prize winner have been seen enjoying a drink in Sandy Bells. Neither is it unusual to see musician Cathal

Mc Connell, all Ireland flute & whistle champion of Boys of the Lough, John Martin of Tannahill Weavers, Mike Katz of the Battlefield Band, folk singer Andy Chung and musician John Sampson in Sandy Bells among other fine professional musicians who enjoy a dram there and on occasion will play.

A respected and well kept unofficial rule in Sandy Bells has always been that when famous personalities enter the bar they are left in perfect peace to enjoy their drink and customers would never contemplate disturbing them to ask for an autograph or to take a photograph.

Over the years, the part time bar staff have come from very wide backgrounds and have represented countries including Italy, France, Australia, Ireland, England, Canada and the United States of America.

Mike Katz, Peter McClements and John Martin
@ G Ferguson

Currently, there are over twenty regular session musicians who play in Sandy Bells. Among them are fiddler Kathryn Nicoll, a past winner of the Glenfiddich Spirit of Scotland music award, fiddlers Peter McClements and Adam Jack recorded on the Sandy Bells Ceilidh, songwriter, blues and county musician, Ewan Forfar, guitarist Chick McAulay, flutist/guitarist Tom Oakes and Duncan McInnes and Gordon Turnbull from the group Cauldstane Slap which formed in Sandy Bells in 2011. Fiddler and bass player, Freddie Thomson has continuously encouraged and inspired musicians throughout his 40 years of playing in the bar sessions. If a session is short of a musician Freddie's the man to fix it.

The Sandy Bells official web site was designed and launched at the following address in March 2014 www.sandybellsedinburgh.co.uk. The bar contact details are:

Freddie Thomson, Cathal McConnell, Sharon Creasey
© G Ferguson

telephone: 0131 225 2751, email: sandybellsedinburgh@gmail.com. There are also copious video clips of the bar on U Tube and the web has countless reviews of the pub.

Sandy Bell's is open from 12 noon until 1am Monday to Saturday and Sundays 12.30pm to midnight. Permanent music sessions generally commence around 9pm weekdays and 3pm at weekends with an additional slow fiddle session from 6pm on Mondays, known fondly by the locals as the 'Itchy Scratchy Session'.

The slow fiddle session is followed every second Monday at 7.30pm by the Scots Moothie Group, led by George Current, a former tutor of the Scottish Music Group Moothie class. The session consists of up to 15 harmonica players who are known in the bar as the 'Sookie Blowies' Two or three times a year these two sessions combine to a rousing foot stomping effect.

The Itchy Scratchy Session: oil painting by Gillian Ferguson

The 'Sookie Blowies' Session
© Gillian Ferguson

Fiddles, flutes, mandolins, small pipes, accordions, double bass, guitars, bodhran, and concertinas are just some of the many instruments often played in Sandy Bells along with a piano which was recently added to the bar session area in April 2014. It is said that once even a didgeridoo was incorporated into one of the sessions.

Music can vary between a fiery Galician/Scottish/Irish vibe to a more song-driven session. Folk and blues, as well as the traditional Scottish and Irish jigs and reels, are often played. As with the tradition of Sandy Bells, visiting musicians and singers often join in on some of the sessions or on occasion will strike up an impromptu session. This can include many fine well known professional and international musicians especially during the Edinburgh festival. Anything can happen musically but that has always been the beauty of Sandy Bells ...

Sandy Bells pub sign
© Gillian Ferguson

Appendix 1

CHRONOLOGY

1840s	The commencement of buildings erected in Forrest Road
1874	Robertson, the grocer was at 25 Forrest Road
1921	Last directory entry for Robertson at 25 Forrest Rd
1923/26	25 Forrest Road was occupied by W G McLeod
1926/29	25 Forrest Road premises were known as 'Jacks'
1929	Mrs M. C. Bell became the owner of the Forrest Hill Bar
1947	The Forrest Hill Bar became a medical school retreat Sandy Porter was the Head barman at Sandy Bells
1958	Stuart MacGregor wrote The Sandy Bells Man
1960-1	Mrs Bell sold the bar to Scottish & Newcastle Breweries Sandy Porter retired from being the head barman Johnny MacKenzie became the bar manager Attempts to remove the dividing arch were dashed because of a petition
1970s	STV recorded a documentary at the height of the folk scene Harvey I' Anson became the bar manager

Danish TV recorded a documentary in the bar and the flat at no 47 Forrest Rd.

Harvey Anson retired and Jimmy Cairney became the bar manager

1973   The first issue of Sandy Bells Broadsheet was distributed on 20th August

1974   James Elliot was awarded the Sandy Bells Broadsheet cup

1975   Hamish Henderson was awarded the Sandy Bells Broadsheet cup

1976   Tom Anderson won the Sandy Bells cup

1977   The Sandy Bells Ceilidh was recorded

The Fisher family were awarded the Sandy Bells cup

The Sandy Bells Broadsheet official Tee shirts were put on sale

The Sandy Bells Broadsheet calendar was launched

Sandy Porter was invited to return to Sandy Bells to receive a silver tankard

The Bar license was extended to open between 11am to 11pm

1978   Jimmy Elliot died on 18th February

In May the Jimmy Elliot Memorial Society was formed

16th May performance of the Jimmy Elliot memorial concert in the Usher Hall

From 6-17th August Sandy Bells was closed for redecoration

Topic records were awarded the Sandy Bells Broadsheet Cup in December.

1979   29th May commenced the bar's 50th anniversary celebrations held over 4 days

The Edinburgh Folk Festival's first official press held in Sandy Bells in March

1980   Alex Campbell was awarded the Sandy Bells Broadsheet cup

Jimmy Cairney died on Sunday, 25th May

29th May the bar was closed. 200 people attended Jimmy Cairneys' funeral

1981   Kenny Thomson was awarded the Sandy Bells Broadsheet cup

1982   A fruit machine was installed in the bar and jettisoned into the street

13th September saw the final issue of the Sandy Bells Broadsheet

1987   Charley Woolley became the licensee of the bar

1990s   The Forrest Hill Bar's name was officially changed to Sandy Bells

2002   Hamish Henderson's bust was displayed on the top of the gantry bar in Sandy

2005   Sandy Bells bar won the McEwen's Session Venue of the year.

2007   Charlie Woolley retired after 20 years and Tam Bird became the licensee

Phil Cunningham, Aly Bain and Barbara Dickson; filmed by the BBC the bar

2008   The Lonely Planet Guide cites Sandy Bells as one of the top five Edinburgh attractions

2011   In June Steve Hannah replaced Tam Bird as the licensee

2012   STV recorded a Sandy Bells documentary

Antonio Foricone and the cast of Mother Africa were

filmed in Sandy Bells

2013   The outside of the bar was painted blue

2014   On 5th January until 1st February the bar was closed for refurbishment

In March the official Sandy Bells website was launched.

On 17th April a piano arrived to join the sessions

In May the Forrest Hill Bar/Sandy Bells was 75 years old

June saw the completion of the booklet 'The Story of Sandy Bells'

Appendix 2

SELECTED BIOPIC

Ago, Arthur: AKA Wells Fargo died 1981, Singer, and tireless promoter of folk music

Anderson, Tom MBE: Winner of Sandy Bells Cup 1976 and President of TMSA

Arthur, Davy: Former front man of the Irish folk group the Fureys

Bain, Aly MBE: Well known supreme traditional Shetland fiddler

Barclay, Bill: Comedian, Radio/TV presenter, performed free at J Elliot memorial concert

Barrow, Dr John: Editor of Sandy Bells broadsheet and producer of Folk concerts

Bayne, Hamish: Member of the McCalmans folk group

Bell, Mrs M C: First owner of Forrest Hill Bar

Bell, Paddie: Irish singer formally of the Corrie Folk trio

Bell, Sandy: Who knows for sure?

Bells Chorus: Regulars of Sandy Bells in good voice recorded on the Sandy Bells Ceilidh

Bennet, Martyn: Died 2005. Scottish musician performed at world premiere of Braveheart

Bird, Tam: Former licensee of Sandy Bells until 2011

Bogle, Eric: Folk singer/writer of 'No Mans' Land' and 'the band played Waltzing Matilda'

Bothy Band, The: Traditional Scottish folk band

Boys of the Lough: Internationally known Irish Celtic band

Brennan, Mike: Irish musician and stalwart of folk music

Broderick, Mick: Drummer and vocalist in the Whistlebinkies

Broon, Jock: Played tenor banjo on the Sandy Bells Ceilidh

Burns, Alex: Stalwart of folk music and folk/blues guitarist

Burns, Robert: Former barman and member of Sandy Bells Chess Club

Cairney, Jimmy: Manager of Forrest Hill bar from earl 1970s to 1980; died 25 May 1980

Campbell, Alex: Musician/ambassador of folk music. 1980 Winner of the Sandy Bells cup

Campbell, Donald: 1950's member of Edinburgh Folk Song Society

Chalmers, Norman: Multi musician who played the concertina on Sandy Bells Ceilidh

Chieftains, The: Internationally known Irish folk group and winner of six Grammy awards

Chandler, Geoff: Well-known chess player and member of the Sandy Bells Chess team

Chorda: Folk Musicians, John Croall, Norman Chalmers, Peter McClements, Rod Paterson

Chung, Andy: Popular folk singer and entertainer from Fife

Clancy's, The: Irish folk band originally brothers, Tom, Pat and Liam

Clark, Alistair: Of Scotsman Publications and winner of Sandy Bells cup in 1979

Connolly, Billy: Internationally known TV personality, folk singer and comedian

Cowans, The: A folk group who offered free service to ease financial strain on SBB

Crichton-Smith, Ian: Prolific author of poetry, novels, short stories and novels. Died 1998

Croall, John: Musician/singer in Jock Tamsons Bairns, bodhran player/Sandy Bells Ceilidh

Cruikshanks, Liz and Maggie: Sisters who sang traditional Scottish folk songs together

Cullin, Harry: In the Danish TV documentary. Became the manager of the Oxford Bar

Current, George: Harmonica player who leads the moothie sessions

Cunningham, Phil MBE: Recognised as Scotland's foremost accordion player

Cunningham, Johnny: Deceased singer of Silly Wizard/ Touchston/Nightnoise.

Davidson. John: Folk banjo player, died 25 November 1976

De Dannan: Well-known Irish folk music group of four musicians

Dickson, Barbara: Internationally known singer who started her singing in Sandy Bells

Donaldson, Alistair 'Ali': Deceased 2013. Musician of Silly Wizard

Drever, Kris: Singer and guitarist of groups Fine Friday and Lau formed in Sandy Bells

Dubliners, The: Internationally known Irish folk band

Eaglesham, Bobby: Scottish folk singer/ musician of Five Hand Reel who died in 2004

Easy Club, The: Members: John Martin, Rod Patterson, Jock Evans, Norman Chalmers

Edwards, Len: Magician and inventor of the Sandy Bell Shuffle card trick

Elliot, Jimmy: First winner of the Sandy Bells cup in 1974. Died 18th February 1978

Fisher, Archie MBE: Singer, songwriter of the Fisher family and Radio Scotland presenter

Fisher Family: Well known Folk singing family – Archie, Ray, Cilla, Cindy, Joyce, Audrey

Fisher, Ray: Singer with brother Archie brought the family to the attention of the public

Forcione, Antonio: Guitarist/composer, filmed in Sandy Bells

Flemming, Chuck: Former fiddler in JSD Band and Trees

Fletcher, Brittonie: Photographer of current Sandy Bells worthies and current barmaid

Frier, Tich: Scottish folk singer, songwriter and humorist

Fraser, Alfie: Played bodhran in Sandy Bells sessions

Furey, Finbar: Irish singer and musician of the Furey's folk group

Furey, Paul: Deceased 2002. Irish singer/musician of the Fureys/Buskers/Brendan Leeson

Grant, Iain: Piper Major, harmonica player who played in bar sessions for many years.

Gaughan, Dick: Well known singer of Scottish traditional ballads and 'muckle' songs

Gavin, Frankie: Folk fiddler of De Dannan.

Gray, Muriel: Well known Scottish author, broadcaster and journalist

Gilllane, Roy: From the Tannahill Weavers

Green, Ian: Sandy Bells broadsheet editor, founder of Fuzz Folk and Greentrax recordings

Greenan, Jimmy: Deceased. Offered free service to ease financial strain on SBB

Greentrax Recordings: Front runner of recordings among Scottish labels

Hamilton, Geordie: Writer and regular performer in Sandy Bells

Hannah, Steven: Licensee of Sandy Bells from June 2011

Hardie, Ian: Multi instrument musician/composer of Chorda, fiddler Sandy Bells Ceilidh.

Harris, Emmylou: American international singer and song writer.

Henderson, Hamish: Died 2002, intellectual/song writer/and mentor of folk music.

Hill, Bill: Writer, broadcaster, songwriter who performed free to ease financial strain on SBB

Hoy, Derek 'Happy': Fiddler, Jock Tamsons Bairns and Bella McNab Dance Band. d. 2012

I'Anson, Harvey: Manager of Sandy Bells in the mid 1960's to the early 1970's

Idle, Eric: TV personality, actor and original member of Monty Python

Imlach, Hamish: Famous Scottish folk singer, entertainer and raconteur who died in 1996

Jack, Adam: Fiddler and former vocalist with Chorda. Still regularly plays in the bar

James, John: Guitarist and songwriter

Jansch, Bert: Musician, singer, songwriter founder member of Pentangle who died in 2011

Jock Tamson's Bairns: Scottish traditional music group formed in Sandy Bells in 1970s

Johnston, Calum: Singer of Gaelic songs at the Theatre workshop in 1940's. Deceased

Johnson, "Peerie" Willie: Well-known jazz, blues and folk musician

Johnston, Allan: Guitar player on Sandy Bells Ceilidh and composer

Katz, Mike: Piper in the Battlefield Band

Kennedy, Nuala: Vocalist/flute player in the group Fine Friday formed in Sandy Bells

Kyle, Danny: Scottish folk singer and songwriter who died in 1998

Lochead, Liz: 1950s singer in Sandy Bells and member of Edinburgh Folk Song Society

MacColl, Ewan: 1915-89. Folk singer/songwriter/actor/poet, playwright, record producer

MacDiarmid, Hugh: Famous Scottish poet who died in 1978

MacGregor, Stuart Dr: Deceased writer of the Sandy Bells Man and The Myrtle and Ivy

MacKenzie,Johnny: Manager of The Forrest Hill Bar in 1960s

McBeath, Jimmy: Died 1972. Singer of Bothy ballads/accomplished pipe/ accordion player

McCalmans, The: Successful folk group: Ian McCalman, Derek Moffat and Hamish Bayne

McClements, Peter: Current session fiddler of the Sandy Bells Ceilidh and Chorda

Mc Connell, Cathal: All Ireland flute and whistle champion of Boys of the Lough.

McCormick, Malcolm: Cartoonist appointed to many Scottish and national newspapers

McCoy, Kenny (Newkie'): Music Kenny McCoy's farewell to Sandy Bells dedicated to him

McGinn, Matt: Deceased 1977. Author/ poet/ folk singer influential in folk music

McKidd, Kevin: International actor with parts in Trainspotting, Rome and Grays Anatomy

McLean, Dougie: Folk musician in Sandy Bells sessions

McLean, Sorley: Significant Scottish poet. Died 1996 age 86

McLeod, Kitty and Marietta: Scottish Traditional Gaelic folk singers in 1940's

McLeod, Tash: Caricaturist in Sandy Bells Broadsheet

McManus, Tony: Fine Celtic guitarist and teacher

McNeil, Flora MBE: Gaelic singer discovered 1950's by Alan Lomax/Hamish Henderson

Martin, John: Fiddler in well-known folk group, Tannahill Weavers.

Menuhin, Sir Yehudi OM, KBE: World famous violinist

Milne, Jimmy: Performed in Sandy Bells and lived in the flat nearby

Moffat, Derek: Deceased member of the McCalmans folk group

Moore, Eilish: Irish folk singer who sang on the Danish TV documentary at 47 Forrest Rd

Munro, Neil: Teacher, guitarist and composer

Murray, Jessie: Sang 'muckle' or big songs in the 1950's in Sandy Bells

Nicoll, Kathryn: Accomplished fiddler who currently plays in Sandy Bells.

Noakes, Rab: Singer/songwriter. Singer on the Danish TV documentary at 47 Forrest Road

Paterson, Rod: Exponent of Burn's songs and bass player in Sandy Bells Ceilidh

Paxton, Tom: American folk singer/ songwriter/guitarist. Wrote 'the last thing on my mind'

Peatbog Fairies, The: Successful Celtic fusion band formed in 1994

Planxty: Well-known traditional Irish folk band

Porter, Sandy: Head barman at the Forrest Hill Buffet until 1960

Rafferty, Gerry: D. 2001. Singer/song writer, of the Humblebums who Recorded Baker St

Redpath, Jean MBE: Traditional folk singer and preeminent interpreter of Burns song.

Rievers, The: Pop band from Texas 1984-1991 who reformed in 2008

Ritchie, Jean: Appalachian folk traditional singer who plays lap dulcimer

Robertson, Jeannie MBE: Well known Scottish folk singer who died age 90 in 1968

Roxton, Keith: A member of Sandy Bells chess team

St Clair, Isla: TV presenter, actress and folk singer inspired by Jeannie Robertson

Seeger, Pete: Famous American folk singer and champion of causes died in 2014 aged 94

Shooglenifty: Edinburgh based six piece Celtic fusion band founded in 1990

Silly Wizard: Scottish folk band formed in 1970's well known throughout Europe

Smith, Rob: Composer of the Sandy Bells Hornpipe

Stevenson, Anna-Wendy: fiddler/singer of Fine Friday group formed in Sandy Bells

Stewart, Belle: Folk singer known for a vast repertoire of traditional folk songs

Stott, Ken: Well known folk singer and guitarist

Strachan, John: Sang 'muckle' songs in Sandy Bells during the
1950's

Tannahill Weavers: One of Scotland's premier and international
trailblazer folk bands

Thomson, Freddie: Fiddler/double bass player/inspiration of
music for 40 years in Bells

Thomson, Kenny: Journalist: Chaired Edinburgh Folk Club.
Sandy Bells cup winner 1982

Topic Records: Winners of Sandy Bells cup in 1978

Ward, Tom: Frequented Sandy Bells and lived in flat nearby

Watt, John: Songwriter, singer, raconteur: Champion of Scottish
folk and traditional music

Weavers, The: An American folk quartet folk led by Pete Seeger.
Disbanded 1952

Weatherstone, Jock: Folk musician, offered free service to ease
financial strain on SBB

Whellans, Mike: Currently one man blues band and former
member of Boys of the Lough

White, Tam: Blues singer who made his musical debut in a skiffle
group in Sandy Bells

Wiedenhof, Michael: Multi skilled musician and current head
barman

Woolley, Charlie: Licensee of Sandy Bells from 1987 to 2007

Appendix 3

SOME OF THE MUSICIANS PLAYING IN SANDY BELLS SESSIONS 2014

Adam Jack, Anna Smith, Carrie Thomas, Cathy Sharpe, Chick Macaulay, Duncan McInnes, Ewan Forfar, Freddie Thomson, Gordon Turnbull, Jack Badcock, Kathryn Nicol, Kenny, Michael Gill, Nigel Richard, Peter McClements, Peter Thoumie, Robert Chalmers, Tom Oakes.

Current bar session: Guitarist, Ewan Forfar and fiddler, Adam Jack
© Ian Ferguson

Appendix 4

<u>NOTES</u>

Bothy Ballards	Characterised by directness and simplicity of rural Scotland
Ceilidh, Kaillie	An entertainment of traditional Scottish music and dance
Crack, craic	Talk, gossip: an entertaining talker/conversation: (Irish:craic)
Dram	A rough measure of whisky
Darien Scheme	To colonise the Isthmus of Panama. Resulting in losses of nearly quarter to half the money circulating in Scotland
Edinboro, Embro	Edinburgh
Edinburgh Festival	World's largest annual arts festival: August for three weeks
Flodden Wall, The	A 16th century Edinburgh city defensive city wall built following the Scots defeat in battle of Flodden in 1513
Gantry, Gauntry, Gauntress	A spirit stand behind the bar in a Scottish public house
Howf, Houf	A favourite haunt or meeting place often a public house

Local, The	Usually a public house used frequently
Locals/regulars	Frequent customers in a bar
Moothie	A mouth organ/harmonica
Puggie	Commonly a fruit or gambling machine
School of Scottish Studies	Founded by the University of Edinburgh in 1951
Reikei, Reekie	Auld Reekie means Old Smokey a name for Edinburgh
Telfer Wall, The	A 1620 extension to the Flodden wall named after mason, John Taillefer. Both walls controlled trade, taxes and smuggling

SELECTED BIBLIOGRAPHY

Brandwood, Geoff. The History and Heritage of the Public House: English Heritage 2004

Bruce, Tom. Rebus's Favourite: The Deuchars Guide to Edinburgh Pubs Orion Publishing 07

Clark, Alistair, Aly Bain; Fiddler On The Loose: Mainstream Publishing Edinburgh 1993

Edinburgh and Leith Post Office Directories from 1869. Murray and Gibb Edinburgh

Foster, Allan: The Literary Traveller in Edinburgh. Mainstream Publishing Edinburgh 2005

Fraser, Bashabi: Edinburgh an Intimate City. City of Edinburgh Council, 2000

Grant, James: Cassell's Old and New Edinburgh Volume IV

Green, Ian. Fuzz to Folk – Trax of My Life: Luarth Press 2011

History and Derivation of Edinburgh Street Names. City of Edinburgh Corporation 1975

MacGregor, Stuart. The Myrtle and Ivy: M MacDonald Edinburgh 1967

Pocket Scots Dictionary: Polygon at Edinburgh 1988

Raising the Bar: An Introduction to Scotland's Historic Pubs.: Historic Scotland 2012

Sandy Bells Broadsheets issues from Aug 1973 to September 1982

Sandy Bells Broadsheet Calendar 1979

Scottish Folk Music.com

Slaughter, Michael. Scotland's True Heritage Pubs. Campaign for real ale 2007

The Campaign for Real Ale site (CAMBRA)

The Edinburgh Evening News 26 Nov 2000 to 22 December 2001

The Royal Commission on the Ancient Historical Monuments of Scotland: Canmore Site

The Scotsman Newspaper Group issues from 2000 onwards

Thomson, James U: Edinburgh Curiosities: Birlinn Ltd 2004

Thomson, Ken. Article, Harmony Bar

West, Gary. Voicing Scotland. Luarth Press Edinburgh 2013

The author has excluded web sites that tend to be ephemeral or of varying accuracy.

THE AUTHOR

Gillian Ferguson was born in Devon in 1946 and grew up in Greater London before moving to Scotland in 1967. Currently residing in Edinburgh and winner of 16 amateur painting awards, in her spare time she enjoys writing for pleasure. This is her first publication.

Lightning Source UK Ltd.
Milton Keynes UK
UKOW06f1606300714